D1021386

# RECKLESS CONSTELLATIONS

# RECKLESS
# CONSTELLATIONS

BY GRANT
CLAUSER

Cider Press Review
San Diego

Cider Press Review
PO BOX 33384
San Diego, CA, USA
ciderpressreview.com


First edition
10 9 8 7 6 5 4 3 2 1 0

ISBN: 9781930781511
Library of Congress Control Number: 2017963560
Cover photo "Toyah Texas" by Jason Weingart, JASONRWEINGART.COM
Author photograph by Susan Clauser
Book design by Caron Andregg

Printed in the United States of America
at Bookmobile in Minneapolis, MN USA.

*People will hold us to blame.*

—David Bowie, "We Are the Dead"

*for Dod, Shelly, Jim and all the ghosts.*

# CONTENTS

## Part 1

Confessions of a Snipe Hunter / 3

Stealing Clay from the Crayola Factory / 4

Holding on to an Electric Fence / 6

Burning Down the Carousel / 8

The Neighbor Killed Snakes / 10

Lucky / 11

Midnight / 12

After the Tree Fort Fire / 13

Trigger Warning / 15

The Breakfast Club / 16

Difference / 17

Reckless Constellations / 18

Nazareth Road / 19

Slasher / 20

Hexenkopf Hill Road / 22

With Shelly at the Goodwill / 23

Villanelle for the Allentown Punk Rockers'
    30-Year Reunion / 24

Snapper / 25

Fishing with Ghosts / 26

Reunion / 27

Memorious / 28

Going Back / 30

# Part 2

Coat of Arms / 33
To Read Dead Poets / 35
If This is All We Have / 36
Coasting / 37
To My Young Daughters When They're Older / 38
All Winter / 40
Crossing the Lake with Natalie / 41
Dog's First Spring / 42
All Summer / 43
Doppler Effect / 44
Ode to My Old Brown Boots / 45
Bluegill / 47
Cow Tipping / 49
Slant Six / 51
Ignition / 52
Ode to Scrapple / 53
Snakeskin / 55
The Old Ways / 56
Fairy Stories I Forgot to Tell You / 58
Elegy for My Daughter's Toy Unicorn / 60
World's End Revisited / 61
Too Late / 63

# Part 3

History Lessons  / 67

Elegy for the Lehigh Thermometer Works, 1945  / 68

Thing She Couldn't Let Go of  / 70

Songs for the Donated Dead  / 72

Cliff  / 73

Autumn Madness  / 75

Ghost Barn  / 77

Ode to the Half-dead Bear on the Way to Defiance  / 78

Catch and Release  / 79

Ode to Mutts  / 80

To A Friend on the Loss of Her Son  / 81

Elegy for a Broken Sump Pump  / 84

Sight Casting  / 86

Elegy for a Bounced Check  / 87

Camouflage  / 89

Mapping Mars  / 91

Ode to Hellgrammites  / 92

First Steps  / 94

Tumble Brook  / 95

Final Poem (Trail Head)  / 96


Acknowledgments  / 97

# ONE

# Confessions of a Snipe Hunter

It is all about the dark,
the useless call,
the flashlight shining
in a paper bag
like a will-o-wisp
guiding through a swamp,
and eventually we learn,
the way we learn
most in life,
through failure and trickery
that it's the dark that matters
when we step out of trust
and into the small illumination
of imagination,
the way the farthest stars
can only be seen
on the darkest nights,
the hope that somewhere
out in the dense forest
there's something else
trusting and foolish enough
to enter your small light.

# STEALING CLAY FROM THE CRAYOLA FACTORY

Bushkill Creek churned past
the old plant where
every Wednesday
the foreman filled a bin
with modeling clay
that didn't measure up.
Kenny and I crept in
after the second shift workers
poured their thermoses
out on the lot and drove home.
We stood on barrels or crates
to reach the big trough
where blocks of clay
dropped from a chute all day
and melted into boulders
from red to gray.
Heaving handfuls
over the side, one would fill
a sack while the other mined
for bright finds, greens and yellows,
the blues that looked like new
denim or the sky
reflected off the Bushkill dam.
Done, we'd squeeze back
under the fence, leave
some blood on the wire
or a sneaker stuck
back in the clay bin
like a tar-pit tiger,
then bike home with a haul

our friends admired,
and together build volcanoes
filled with baking soda and vinegar.
We'd watch eruptions over and over
until the whole little town
was swallowed in our ash.

# HOLDING ON TO AN ELECTRIC FENCE

On our side, the tree fort and tire swing,
the rock we called home base for tag,
a pond just deep enough for frogs to spawn.

On the other side were horses, swayback nags
swatting flies with their tails, a paint-peeling barn
leaning on its shadows, a truck without wheels.

Dod dared me first, said he'd done it lots of times
and lived, his slant grin mocked me,
and Jenny the Jehovah girl snapped her gum.

She wouldn't come to parties, sat down in class
when we said the pledge to the flag,
raked her nails down the blackboard without flinching.

She spat on my hands first because Dod said
that's best, then I grabbed the wire and tensed,
ready for fire, to smell smoke boil my brains

but just a tingle came, like a limb waking up
after leaning too long on it, I held on
and screamed anyway, scared the shit

out of Dod and Jenny, both swearing
my hair stood up for a moment. But
I knew, and the horses looked on

the way horses do, a thousand pounds
of nothing in their eyes but horseflies, her
bubble gum spit on my hands all day

and every time I brought them to my face,
the electricity returned, the jolt of awakening,
the shock of grabbing something new and holding on.

# BURNING DOWN THE CAROUSEL

was not my idea, but watching paint peel back
from the white horse's strained face thrilled
and shocked like a roller coaster you think is safe
but then realize the operator is blind,

and even then I knew enough about the world
to understand those wooden horses had lives beyond
their worn down saddles, their chipped glass eyes
that lasted longest in the carousel's losing fight

with flames, the calliope hitting its brass death notes
as it collapsed to the floor, smoke stinging our own eyes
where we hid behind the Fun House, its clown face
long fallen or dragged away by vandals

like most everything else at this abandoned park.
The gas and lighter Dod stole from his dad after
he was too drunk to notice, and then we
circled the park for hours, hopping fences,

breaking into the Haunted House where every skeleton
lay smashed already. Spray painted names marked
where older boys lashed out at their youth
or carved their history into fake coffins and ticket booths,

until finally we came to the carousel, leaning hard
on wheels burst from dry rot and years of cotton candy
stuffed riders, the ghosts of children hanging tight trying
to catch the brass ring, a quick wave and hand clap

from mothers beyond the rail. Dod I swear was crying
when he drenched the white stallion with gas, lit the bear

and tiger, then tossed the can into the creek—
the first flames crawling over a silver mane

like a praying mantis looking for the softest tissue
between head and body, where in the last act of love
it plants its mouth, cutting off the head, devouring
the flesh, leaving behind a shell it will soon forget.

# THE NEIGHBOR KILLED SNAKES

Each spring they swarmed the Jehovah woman's garden,
ten or twenty a day, hundreds in the length of a week.

Somewhere from an underground nest, they bust forth
like weeds, bamboo shoots you can't keep down.

And in the afternoon sun, before her daughters
got home from school, she'd chop them

one by one with a shovel, or crush their heads
with the heel of her gardening boots, trouble

their tiny bones into red and blue stains
then leave them for her husband to clean up.

I'd find the strays he missed, broken backs
with their heads still on, tongues forking in and out

and try to save them, take them home, hide
their bloody stripes in the shrubs around our garden

until one day she caught me, told my dad, called me little devil
for stealing, called me sick for playing with death,

said I'd be known as that boy in the neighborhood,
the one always caught with blood on his hands.

# LUCKY

Dod remembers pushing the knife
deep behind the fish jaw
and cutting down to its tail.
If he was lucky he could wrap
his pointing finger around the guts
at the gill and pull them all out
in one feather like when mama
collapsed in the driveway
and said dad won't be back
or anything tonight
then went to her room
and shut herself for three days
until someone called the neighbor.
He remembers thinking that raccoons
must be so lucky
to find these fish guts lying
in the weeds
like a man who finds
his shotgun fully loaded
and everyone asleep.

# MIDNIGHT

There's no good explanation
for what we did back then
driving to the cemetery
before the *Rocky Horror*
*Picture Show,* stoned and pumped
on midnight at the grave
of a girl we never knew,
daughter of a cult leader
or a coven, we'd heard tell.
And nearby the plot
my own grandfather lay
where we placed him
years before, last
of six brothers to die.
I remember the winter oak trees
gripping the moon like a fist
trying to keep a catfish
from escaping.
No one would admit fear
but Dod lit a candle quick.
We looked over our shoulders
and with a schnapps toast
poured on the ground,
ran back to the car.
Cop headlights came
up the hill. Dod tried
to toss the weed.
A garden of dead all around us
And no good excuse
on our ready lips.

# After the Tree Fort Fire

Some things are better off in flames,
better seen in blaze with a fall wind
stirring sparks and leaves of nearby trees
curled into lobster claws from the heat.
Board by broken board
we nailed wood to wood, clung
to moss on the big oak and sycamore
until we had a floor, roof, plywood
walls and a ladder nailed crosswise
like stitches up the tree side
to reach the door. And now nothing.
Gone to fire—my tape deck
that played Molly Hatchet into sunset.
Gone the dumpster dive rugs we tacked
to the floor, the raccoon nest routed
one winter, the box of Trojans
for just in case you'd talk Dee
into following you down the deer path
to the woods. Beer cans, Boone's Farm
and Mad Dog Orange Jubilee empties
piled in the corner or broken
on the rocks below. And then you,
found swinging one day from a rope
you made, feet a man's length
from the ground though barely more
than a boy's life worn into your brow.
And I hear when they found you there,
our tree fort creaking from the weight
you threw, the leaves had just started turning
as their chlorophyll redrew the season,
orange and red revealed under all that green,

as if the reason for holding out all summer
was just to be part of fall's grand parade.
So now it's burned, our own scorched earth
promise to leave a mark on land that mattered,
to matter enough that someone looked up
at night and saw a fire, that fire is the last
resort when you've pulled out all the nails
that hold a thing together, and in the ashes
left behind, the thing that lingers
is the hole, a cold gap among the trees.

# Trigger Warning

Dod had his father's pistol
again. Shelly was drunk
but not too much
for a school night.
Her face the soft flush
of poison ivy.
The car window that wouldn't roll
all the way up
let rain in, but smoke out.
Lights shone from the Indian Tower
so we drove to the bowling lanes.
The parking lot lamps
made circles in the asphalt
like crop circles
and we were alien species.
I think back now
about how Shelly
slammed the car door,
and everyone watched her walk
the way eyes follow a train
running off its tracks.
Her hair wet on her face
as she entered the building.
Dod telling me to drive
anywhere the hell out of here.

# THE BREAKFAST CLUB

The year everything changed
like a volcano the town knew about

but built on anyway, we drove
River Road with the headlights off.

Maybe it started at the drive-in.
When Shelly stood on the hood

of my Dodge Dart and threw bottles
back at the face of Judd Nelson because

black boots and king snake eyebrows
can bring out the best in some people.

Under the concession stand the husks
of dried moths swirled in a dust devil.

We walked to the canal, threw rocks
as far as we could at the locks,

and came back wet with mud
on our jeans and ferns in our shoelaces.

A month later she came back
from the clinic, eyes slack like curtains

drawn over the front window
so no one knows who's home.

# DIFFERENCE

She said it's important to know
the names of trees,
the difference between
one spidered leaf
and the next,
then I think about how
many kinds of rain
can fall over the roof,
how both snow
and summer hurricanes
can make the river rise,
how you call something love
even when it isn't,
and when Eve held
an apple out to Adam
he didn't ask, "braeburn
or red delicious?"

# Reckless Constellations

After leaving Old Pat behind
the liquor store, we crossed
the state line back to River Road,
stopped at Devil's Half Acre
where the girls waited with a bonfire
casting a honey glow into trees.

And there around the fire pit
Dod spilled his whiskey lies.
Jim tossed firecrackers in the flames
like mercenaries for spite
and made Shelly jump
back more than once.

When we turned away
from the heat, our breath froze
in front of our faces
the way evening stands still
on some nights, especially
for the young.

Someone danced
until the batteries died
and then all the beer bottles
Old Pat got us lay in reckless
constellations in the woods.
Sparks from the fire rose
with smoke—stars too small
to be named.

# Nazareth Road

At the end of my shift
I went to Dod's house
and found him knees down
in the backyard,
his dad screaming,
picking up handfuls of dog shit
and throwing them at him,
Dod taking it like a door
takes slamming, swinging shut
without comment,
a crack starting in the frame.

# SLASHER

Watching *Friday the 13th*
at Shelly's house, first time alone,
since the rehab, anxious teens
with our hands, like the movie couple,
willing to dive into the lake naked,
daring the script to make us victims,
walk into the monster's maw.
Everyone knew the secret
to survival was staying out
of the woods, but we charged
ahead to the chainsaw's grind.

We watched the whole movie
in our underwear because
her parents weren't home
and no one back then had AC.
My eyes followed the cuts
on her arms the way you follow
train tracks, not knowing
which direction the engine
is coming from, if you're going
down the distant tunnel
or coming back out of it.

She took her shirt off first.
The basement sofa smelled
of mildew and dog and Shelly's perfume.
Caution always loses
in a contest with bare skin.
When a knife cuts you open
there's a moment you want to laugh

at the surprise of it all, the copper penny
smell of blood when you bit
your tongue so hard
you tasted wire for days
and somehow Shelly's hair
was always in my mouth.

# HEXENKOPF HILL ROAD

They say the witch lived in a cave,
or maybe a house that's just a fallen tomb
of stones now fading in the twilight,
or maybe it was a Lenape girl, called Delaware,
who died with a curse on her lips
as she ran from a white hunter
right here, beer cans spilling
out of the Gremlin where we take turns
in the driver's seat,
a week before graduation,
no hands on the wheel, no feet on the gas,
Jim, who will die on a motorcycle
in less than a year, and Dee,
who swears her father doesn't hit her hard,
while thrilled and a little scared
we feel the car start to roll
forward, up the Hexenkopf hill,
the dirt road heading west
into the night, the last sun
down the hill setting behind us,
and we argue if the car
is being pushed or pulled,
sending us away or drawing us in.

# WITH SHELLY IN THE GOODWILL

*Replace the white laces*
*with red,* she said, *and this corset*
*is almost punk enough to wear.*
We play the daydream game
some more, try on jackets
of the dead, take practice steps
in someone else's shoes,
trade rags for rags,
and arrange the living room décor
to suit our mood—
an imagined house we'd share
with dogs and other strays.
We set the table
for a feast, gather
all the empty candle holders
and mime their flames,
pretend our friends
are here and whole, a home
that's real enough to stay.
Finally, Shelly takes the old viola
and bows a sonata
only we can hear,
like the music birds make
when they abandon their nests
for the winter.

# Villanelle for the Allentown Punk Rockers' 30-Year Reunion

Frank Feinberger is dead.
Jules turns hot dogs on the charcoal grill.
The music's too loud to hear what she said.

What's left of the band bob their heads
as we share stories, photos of kids until
she repeats that Frank Feinberger is dead.

She points out fading tattoos, our punk cred
stretched over arms and backs, names misspelled,
I shout because the music's too loud to hear what she said.

They found him at home, OD'd and naked
with a short note and a bag of pills.
It's true that Frank Feinberger is dead.

It's true Tom's an accountant—he got ahead.
Sheri's a hair dresser. Jet pays her bills.
I turn to the music's to avoid what she said.

Adam's a waiter. Tina died in a birthing bed.
Meat is burning on the charcoal grill.
She writes on my hand: *Frank Feinberger is dead*
'cause I don't want to live with words that she said.

# Snapper

The edges are hazy now, but I still remember the ice cream smudge
on your cheek as we fought in the car, a fleck of sweetness only
an hour old,  dried and needing to be wiped away. Your scent,
cigarettes and mall perfume, filled the front seat, and when you
slammed the door to leave, the tape deck startled off, too obvious
a metaphor. I could have apologized then, could have followed you
across the parking lot, changed it all. My teenage brain a marsh
of indecision, birds rising in all directions, and in the cold mud a
snapping turtle patiently waiting for flesh. I went off to college, you
from checkout counter to assistant manager and then who knows.
There's a reason the heart is in the center of the body. As it rises to
speak it gets stuck in the throat, cuts off the air, makes blood vessels
swell. I know it wouldn't have mattered, but back in the marsh
birds still gather to their separate tribes, fan their nests with wings
that have seen miles of sun on one side and shadow on the other.
The snapping turtle has grown hard and gray, fat with all the small
things it chokes down.

# Fishing with Ghosts

Lowlands around the creek
are all jack-in-the-pulpit and fern.
Dod arranges rocks into a circle,
raises a fire from ash we left behind.

The salamanders we caught as kids are gone.
So is the smell of honeysuckle,
but the honeysuckle still grows
like a fog rolling down the hill.

I say something about Jim.
His silver motorcycle and white helmet.

Our lines sparkle over the small dam
but no trout rise.

He says something about the good old days
before every memory had a dead person standing in the doorway.

I say good old days are paint on an old shed
where we keep the tools, ax and shovel,
that bike rusting against a rotting wall,
things we need sometime.

# REUNION

We sit at the table in your mother's kitchen, the world's worst coffee cooling in a pot between us. It's only been a few years, but seems like more. One of us traces the table's wood grain with a finger. The other remembers fingers on a face, tracing ears, chin. It's a short visit. The kind of check-in you know will be the last, will have to cover long distances and hold despite the gaps, like the stone walls of a farmhouse long since fallen into rubble and vines. A stranger finds it in the wood and feels the stories once lived there, some heat still clinging to the hearth stone's soot. You mention Dod and Jim, say the the woods we knew are new houses already, the lights of families streaming from windows where our bonfires once made dervish shadows on the trees. How hard it must have been to build there, our ground just weak shale, the topsoil a myth settlers here believed was hope. What we miss most is not the days or nights, but how we felt about them, how you could stand on the slope where the cemetery met the creek and hear every shifting murmur in the water's way. How ghosts are like keys you've lost, but give up searching for. In an hour someone opens a door, someone offers an embrace, and the sound of a deadbolt sliding shut echoes for longer than it should.

# MEMORIOUS

Some days in spring
the moon hangs around
long after its light
should have gone out.
Dogs bark from farther off
than I should be able to hear.
Senses that trigger regrets—
the meat factory my daughter
hates because she sees
trucks pulling down the road,
pink snouts and haunches
pushing through metal slats,
hundreds of them, the smell
of their rendering travels
from smokestacks two miles away.
It's then I remember
what Dod told me in 1985,
how he stumbled once
upon the off boy, the one
kids picked on since grade school
and because no one was around
he tripped him, then stood above him,
fists and threats and something unknotted
in both of them until the off boy,
16 or 17 at the time, cried
and peed himself there on the street.
Dod left him and asked me later
if I thought the boy had told.
I said no, he's probably used to it,
and we both forgot, smoked our joints
and dangled our legs off a bridge

over a river that ran
over rocks, that carried pebbles
and silt and the moon's reflection
to someplace neither of us
had ever been
or ever planned to go.

# Going Back

Going back to the wreckage
was, of course, a mistake,
like going back for revenge
or digging up the bones
of your childhood pet.
It's not the memory
you find, not the broken
plates and picture frames
vibrating in the rubble,
but the loss of this, like a swarm
of bees you can't run away from
because the more you swat
them from your face,
the deeper they wound,
yet still you believe
you can taste the honey
in their sting.

# Two

# Coat of Arms

If we weren't peasants
our coat of arms would hang
above a great family hearth
instead of crumbled
in the junk drawer
with old cell phone cords
and broken corkscrews.
Instead of swords crossed
for valor, ours would show rusted blades
from the lawnmower that needs fixing.
Our family motto would be
a heavy sigh at dinner
after the children have left,
the sound eyelids make
when they half close
at the end of a sentence
so you know the conversation
is over.
Our coat of arms would bear the wag
of restless dogs,
the cries of mocking birds
and the silence of cars
leaking oil in the driveway.
No one would wear it
on armor or a shield
into battle or a flag
flown over a keep,
but our arms carry it now
like groceries from car
to kitchen cupboard.
We feel it always

like a dancer walking home
from the practice studio,
blisters and tape
on her feet,
pain and pride
bound together.

# TO READ DEAD POETS

is to prepare my grandmother's
recipe for apple something,
to pause my finger for a moment
over the faded lines she wrote
years ago, stained with butter,
then mix the ingredients,
and notice she forgot
to include the measure
of sugar, but my best guess
and the way I remember her house
smaller in winter,
my grandfather padding
from the davenport
to the table,
is as close
as I can get
to the taste I want
to tell my daughters about.

# IF THIS IS ALL WE HAVE

Even infants in the womb
yawn when they're bored,
so when the curtains close
on my daughter's high school play
I'm thinking instead
of woods, some moss I once
held between my fingers,
a newt netted in the green.
And when she asked
me later about her scene, how
Elizabethan she looked, I told her
I was the loudest one clapping
in the seats, rows of parents sharing
praise for love as much as theater—
so if joy in others is all we have
then take it, no matter why,
because a light stretching
under the warm pulse of a mother
doesn't need to hear the heartbeat
like a yawn contagious one to another,
to know everything important
is always within reach.

# COASTING

We're coasting down the hill
like two barrels on a waterfall.
Afternoon insects flick
off our bike helmets and sunglasses.
I'm ahead, rounding the turn
fast, looking for sticks, trash
or any obstacles she'd miss
in her newfound joy for speed.
Isn't this what a father does?
Recon the world so they
can run? Explore the dark
beyond the flashlight's
D-cell glow?
It's not always so easy.
Sometimes bikes collide.
Sometimes the heart is on
the wrong side of the body,
and half our best efforts
become a choice
between one poverty and another.
At the bottom, she gives me
the thumbs up sign
as we pause to look around
at wildflowers
spreading along the path.
I know my road is always uphill,
back the way we came,
but there's no retracing those steps.
The sun behind the trees is broken.

# To My Young Daughters
# When They're Older

Someday you'll be older, and
I hope remember to turn the clocks
the right direction home.
It's Sunday once a week, and dinner's
set for any stranger with our name.

We'll keep your room in order,
every doll, photo and heart-shaped
sketch saved to savor later, dried
flowers in a yearbook, walls still
painted the lavender you loved when younger.

I know what you left behind, but
not what you took along.
The times we camped in pine woods?
The rocks we climbed and swam
below the falls? The campfire songs?

My own best memories of youth—
fields behind the house, the tree
I climbed that scared my mother silly,
father pulling rowboats across a lake
with hope, though every lake was empty.

It's good to sit alone with clocks ticking,
their hands still moving though the batteries leak.
You'll set your own alarms and still be
late, thinking what's important hasn't
happened yet. It's true until it's over.

We can't build memories for the future,
though we try, like building snowmen
you know won't last. Just don't forget
to set your clocks. We say *fall back*
because we're always there to catch you.

# ALL WINTER

Snow whispered the engine
of an old Buick in a field,
its cracked tires stuck in ice.
Some quiet moments interrupted
by yelling and crying.
It was the right amount of snow
or maybe too much
but still the right amount
for most of the year's children
and the old who rarely leave
home anymore—they sit
in the kitchen with their cups.
Crows and cardinals,
the only birds that stayed
unless you count the owls
talking to themselves.
The bare trees in the church woods
seemed to be reaching across
the trails to touch each other.
You remember loving the smell
of chimney smoke, the sound
of train whistles hanging in the cold.
There was yelling and crying.
If not for this, would spring
mean so much?

# CROSSING THE LAKE WITH NATALIE

Don't think of the waves as things
that crash but things you ride.
The water's not as tough as you.
Just lift your paddle high
and stroke hard. Pulling
against wind, the weather boats
were made to break through.
Water is everything behind you
and ahead there's sun and me,
old dad at starboard looking
out for stumps or something
like a branch floating past,
something we missed
the first time out.

# Dog's First Spring

When every scent is new
like birdsong strung
on tree branches
when soft ground
that was hard yesterday
is something that needs
to be thought about
like a sunrise needs
to be thought about
like a rabbit needs
to be chased
because it is a rabbit.

# All Summer

We were surrounded by trees
named after the fruit
they drop. It was the season
of good intentions
ruined by momentum.
Rain brought mosquitoes.
What do they do with all that blood?
Drought shrank the garden
like a bully walking into a playground.
In lawn chairs, after midnight,
we counted meteors with the children.
Metal that fell a million miles
to burn up here.
What's easier to forget—
hope or regret? An easy question.
Better to swat mosquitoes
before they're full,
watch them spill your blood
back on your arm.
Memories, like meteorologists
are unreliable.
We need something solid to save.
On the other hand,
forgetting makes love possible.

# Doppler Effect

Distant stars have their own revolutions
around the universe, their trails
through space alone,
but the suns with planets
circling round them, a mass deep enough
for a warm volcanic hum
will dither, traveling round a path together
through cosmos like two hands linked
at a carnival—the calliope playing
at the center of each cell's thrumming
and here we find them, an irrevocable gravity
in the night, two breaths in a quiet room,
one inhale for each release, one beat
rushing in as the other moves
to fill the space.

# ODE TO MY OLD BROWN BOOTS

I was raised to make things last,
to save the hot pan's bacon grease
in a jar for the next day's fried potatoes,
to rip old shirts in rags for washing
the 15-year-old car.
You've gone almost as far
as my Dodge—from Catesauqua's
asbestos shingled alleys
to the muck bank of the Maumee river.
Every fall I pull you out of the box
and test your soles, wet the leather
with mink oil to keep winter out.
You must know, by now, my path
from garage to gate, the stride
it takes to walk the yard, to round
the pond where thin foxes stalk.
Even burn marks and scuffs
when you stomped an errant spark
or kicked a stone wall loose
can't wear you down.
Your hide's half held up
by blister puss, proof
you made the hike along
Appalachian's rocky spine.
So now it's hard to face
the truth that time's caught up.
No new heel pads can fix
a sole worn that thin.
The black toenail where I dropped
a brick won't grow back strong.
My kids are grown and tall.

They argue like a new world
is on their side, and they're dressed
to walk all over it.
And here you are, stretched and warped,
drying by hearth's wood heat,
emptiness the only thing
that can hold you up.

# BLUEGILL

Say there's a small lake
with a boat dock.
Say the morning's warm,
and the coffee by your side
cools in the shade of pine trees.

Even when light rain
moves in like a dog
settling itself on a rug
you keep casting bobbers
to the rain-pocked lake

because somewhere in the water
between the dark matter
that fills the universe
drift small yellow-gold bellies
and night-blue cheeks.

Now say you remember another lake
with the same cedar-stained water,
your father's arms pulling the rowboat
around periscopic stumps
while your child hands held

the rod, hoping for the gold
he promised was held here,
a whole rich world trembling
at the end of your line
and nothing but a red and white bobber

between you and the years ahead,
dark roads and light,
lakes with sunken stumps or
glass-smooth mornings,
and a line arcing over the distance.

# Cow Tipping

Promise to save your receipts,
to tell the truth on your taxes. Promise
to come to a complete stop at stop signs.
Promise to pay your student loan, to stop
drinking during the week, to always
clean your plate, and turn the lights
out at night. Promise to separate glass from plastic,
to take the old sofa off the porch,
to weed and water the lawn whenever
the neighbor does, but wait until 10 AM
to mow. Promise to take the online survey,
to curb your dog and participate in neighborhood watch.
Pretend you know the mayor's name
and vote in every election. Pretend you don't
wish the mall would slide into the ocean.
Pretend you don't dream
of running through Walmart
setting every yellow sign aflame.
Swear to us. Swear it. Swear to mini vans,
junk mail, a secret stash in the shed,
movie night, Labor day,
vacations at the shore,
inflatable Christmas decorations
and flags in the front yard.
Swear to 30-year mortgages
and tipping the postman.
Swear that never again
will you wander off
into that field,
lay your hands

on their still bodies
and knock the sleeping
cows down.

# SLANT SIX

It was a last ditch effort, and I don't know why
they call it that, but at 92 cutting his chest open
to reach the center muscle couldn't have been
that hard, no pick-ax ditch digger's struggle.

I picture the heart waiting to be touched,
the same one I leaned against as a child
when he rocked me on the porch,
Nana in the yard picking ripe tomatoes.

Parked on Blackberry Alley, his Dodge Dart
collected tree pollen from the neighbor's mulberry
and Catasauqua's bird song wrapping
a summer evening with out-of-sync tunes.

Years later, when eye doctors took his keys
I drove the Dart to Ohio and back,
car held together by chicken wire and Bondo,
slant six powered through winter like a landslide.

I saw him after surgery, hardly a bulge
on the bed, hooked up to machines meant to count
his breaths and beats, assure the nurses death
hadn't passed ICU in the last five minutes.

But it will, and then it did, and when winter came
I drove that car for another year till the dealer
paid me thirty dollars to get it off the road,
the smell of mulberries lingering still.

# IGNITION

Like a museum, the pre-owned lot displays
stories of starts and stops.
Old cars with tires polished black
crack in the sun, their odometers
spun back a few turns on the dial.
We ask about the American truck,
the Japanese sedan, kick the tires
as if that air-filled thud could tell us,
like a palm reading, what kind of luck
these wheels may bring.
I wonder what my father would say,
weighing mileage over years, how long
it takes a thing to reach its peak and then
decline, how they try to hide rust
with cheap paint or mask years
of cigarettes with a dose of something
stronger. My daughter, still hope and wonder,
glides from car to car and pictures herself
on the road, right foot forward
bearing down on the highway
to a place another state away.
When she shifts into drive
the engine answers: *where?*
I try but can't tell her
there's nothing new here,
just new to her.
No matter how old
the keys to the car
are always shiny.

# ODE TO SCRAPPLE

Its name is what was left
when all the better words
were taken for other things.
Here there's title and history,
will to stake a claim
in one word. Scrapple.
I rise early, before the sun
and daughters, before the dog
stretches his old bones
across the door jam
to pee in the dark,
because the economy of dawn
is momentary and true.
The night's crumbs tumbling
into the morning's expectant wag,
and in that crossroad moment
when things become only present,
before either shadow or light
lay claim, I look for compass points
toward the day, plan the route.
Scrapple knows where it comes from
and doesn't mind, wastes nothing
and still keeps it together,
not like me, moving through
the years like a traveler
dropping excess kit
along the trail as the day
heats up.
Let's get righteous about waste,
about taking up what others leave behind.
We build new cities

on the broken walls of the conquered.
We raise our children in the light
of things we've lost,
and still we bury
our dead in green fields.
So dawn I fry the offal, a ponhoss
of cornmeal and pork bones
in butter with eggs,
the dog sniffing around the floor
for bits I've forgotten.

# SNAKESKIN

A snake left its skin on the patio
between a pot of new lavender and another
of thyme not yet grown enough for clipping.
When it's time to shed, a shadow covers
the snake's eyes till the only sense that works
is scent, the forked tongue feeling its way forward.
Late night rain glued the skin to the lavender pot
which tells me the snake dragged itself
across our concrete in the evening, maybe even
while we rocked in the chair swing watching
the sun slide behind the neighbor's oaks,
the snake not knowing we were there.
As light leaked from the day,
a few yellow puddles lingered
evaporating finally in shadows,
and about then the snake,
probably shiny and slick with scales'
first exposure to air, eyes freshly bright
slipped into the garden
leaving its crumpled molt the way
we turn in for the night, leaving the day
and all its stickiness behind.
If only it were that easy, to rise shiny
from sheets in the morning, our skin
unscarred with regrets, and walk
into a garden, our backs warming
under a bright sun, our eyes seeing
finally what's there.

# THE OLD WAYS

Sitting behind the wheel
of a car stuck in snow
falling all around so that
soon the tires will disappear,
the night an old black and white
photo, so that past and present
become just the same picture
and we continue to sit there
watching it, wondering
how we came here, knowing
seasons always return
to their old ways, watching
the owl turn itself around
on a tree limb, wondering
why we only notice owls in winter,
notice in the rear view mirror
how the tracks behind us
fill into the road before us
and watching it happen
seems like the best way
to pass the time, cold
as it is, the air inside the car
is warm, the radio still
picks up a song we liked
in high school,
and in the dark,
we can think of nothing
better than watching
the snow fall, covering
the things we're sure about
along with the things we're not,

learning we can love
each season differently
and believing it's enough,
exactly enough, to let it happen.

# Fairy Stories I Forgot to Tell You

*for my daughter on her 18th birthday*

We heard the witch in the water,
saw the wolf in disguise, the sundry
gods who won their way with promises
hidden in deceits,  seasons pledged
for a few bites of fruit and hell to pay.

Do you remember campfire tales?
Walks in the woods searching for doors
or trails, any sign of tree sprites or things
the hobgoblins left for us to find?
The tracks that dew leaves when it fades.

And in the rivers, creeks that rise
with rain, water nymphs ran under
the downpour catching what the sky
gave up before lighting strikes.
All the worlds that words contain.

That's the thrill, isn't it? That between
each fairy raindrop there's a light, or
at least the chance of one, that you can
catch what you want, let the rest pour
over you, then come back indoors to dry.

If you look around in the right light,
you see all the gods and fairies
you loved or feared, those precious stories
held close at night, the veil held shut
until it's almost out of sight.

I've left out a lot, or held back
stories better saved for other days,
waiting for those days to come.
The ones untold that unfold on their own,
like wildflowers opening overnight.

Prepare the most for those, the surprise
that sunrise brings like trillium
yawning around a hidden spring,
and where the mossy rocks divide
to let the water disappear, that's
the story you were meant to hear.

# ELEGY FOR MY DAUGHTER'S TOY UNICORN

Water in the basement reached the box
of toys. We forget where things are,
what we left to find later. She loved this
and that, and that, but never played
with the brown dog after battery acid
ate through its belly. Day
at the park, play date down the street
with the neighbor who died
in a car accident after we moved away.
We forget her name, but not her long hair.
Years are aspirin that takes away
the sting until you think about pain.
Cobwebs on everything. Wolf spiders.
Centipedes. We want time capsules
instead of memories.
In the box, stuffed bears, compressed
for years, reclaim their shape
when aired out. The colonial doll's leg
where I glued it back turned yellow.
A pink and white unicorn, covered
with blue and gray mold,
will never be the same.

# WORLD'S END REVISITED

*World's End wilderness area,*
*Sullivan County, Pennsylvania*

The trees have aged as much as us
but show it less, their bark turned hard
from fire and the wind that carried songs
down the canyon. When they fall,
their leaves curl up like cast cocoons.

We brought nothing, and took it all home.
Took the wind for granted and the moon
that turned to vapor every morning
and back again to moon. Those stars
that shot the night, burned and gone.

We built for need at the End, loved hot
the way a fire flares in a stone ring
and smolders back to flames in morning.
Dew on our tent evaporated under sun
then down as rain by evening.

No children then, or even dreams
that soon. Now our girls are grown
and moving on to ends they'll choose.
Our choices, work and house, fireplace
in the den, sink dripping in the kitchen.

We've mortgaged more than a house,
our skin and bones. Those days
at World's End, building camp
and fire for the meals, down payment
for the road beyond the river bends.

Everything we've loved stays the same
somewhere, no matter how it's changed.
That's memory. The stones that built
a fire pit, still strong despite
their cracks, hot coals we chose to carry.

# Too Late

If it's true
that the stars we visit
each night as we lie
out here in the grass
died and burned out
millions of years ago
then we are strange mourners
visiting a luminous graveyard,
and the smallness we feel
as we talk about the children
is not distance or wonder
or the shifting perspectives of age,
but the loss of something great
too late to savor.

# THREE

# History Lessons

The gray Mennonite groundskeeper
fumbles a hand truck through the cemetery
replacing headstones that crumbled
past their century,
takes the slabs, their names and dates
worn smooth by years
so even fingers can't decode them,
and stacks them in a pile
in the woods behind the church.
Later he uses some to fix a wall
around a garden,
and one piece sits atop
the septic tank pipe
that lost its cap.
The rest will topple into the creek,
the last shallow letters
of their family names
filled in by silt.

# Elegy for the Lehigh Thermometer Works, 1945

The factory supernova'd
its exit like an A-bomb,
lit the Catasauqua night sky
for hours as it fell beam by beam
into ash and asphalt,
heat enough to melt
glass, let mercury run free
like water to the iron works
next door where tank armor
baked till it glowed.
Nana, as a girl,
ran with the others
to the place she made
thermometers for the war,
leveling quicksilver into glass
to tell the quick from the dying.
All as one, a thousand thermometers
burst their keepers' bonds.
When the second floor crashed
into the first, firefighters
gave up and watched it burn,
using just enough water
to keep the row homes safe.
The whole town's fever
rose like a rebellion.
All the heat they could suffer
in one gold moment
when flames finally reached
the treetops, turned bare limbs

into torches, called every citizen
to witness that enough
was finally enough.

# THINGS SHE COULDN'T LET GO OF

After she lost her leg
in a silk factory accident
when she was seventeen
my grandmother complained
for seventy one years of cold feet
in winter, phantom itches
when August brought mosquitoes
through the broken backdoor.
In her victory garden
she fought the perpetual
weeds that couldn't be stopped
but by digging out the root
like the chickens that kept kicking
after she cut off their heads
until she scooped out the guts.
When we emptied her house
we found a closet filled
with left shoes never worn,
each one stuffed with newspaper
to keep their shape.
The bed she'd shared
with Grandfather leaned
to one side, his body
spooned out a hollow
she avoided for years.
On every table, counter
and drawer, graying photos
saved from before the war,
her long body in long dresses
leaning against black cars
or sitting on front porches,

small feet in pretty shoes.
Under the bed, tied in twine,
letters from a private no one knew,
the last few never opened.

# Songs for the Donated Dead

*"Each year hundreds of people donate their bodies to science in Pennsylvania. And each year, the state board that oversees those donations, the Humanity Gifts Registry, puts on a ceremony to honor those who made that sacrifice."* WHYY Newsworks

They come here every year to sing
to cadavers, arms locked together,
a chorus of doctors giving thanks to bodies
without names, organs they spread open
to rooms of eager students, the unlikeliest choir.

They come every year, invite the families,
if they're known, invite the mayor, arms locked
together, unlikeliest choir, to sing thanks to tissue
samples and the eyeball donor, the car accident,
the lesson on rib removal, skull fracture, rigor mortis.

They spread their arms open, together, the car accident,
the overdoser, those who checked off the box *donor*,
who sing if they're known, unlikeliest choir
to an uncommon audience. Some opened their hearts
for others to hold, rooms of eager students together.

The cadavers sing to an uncommon audience, eager
students of rigor mortise, skull fracture, sons and daughters,
homeless and lovers, a chorus of doctors giving thanks to bodies.
Some opened their hearts. Passed them to others. Unlikeliest choir—
they come here every year to sing to cadavers.

# CLIFF

*A house built too close to a cliff over Lake Whitney in Texas was burned down when it started to fall over the edge.*

*After Jane Hirshfield's "Tree"*

It's foolish to build your house
upon a cliff above a lake

while the earth is still moving
and every star that shines

upon your roof has burned out
its grip on light, and yet

nothing beckons like edges,
a child drawn to balance beams

and your head's desire to lean
over every bridge you cross.

Each morning is a choice between
falling over or stepping back

against a wind that threatens balance
or the desire to spread your arms

and risk what the wind will bring
until there are no choices left,

so when the ground finally slides
enough to pull out from under

what you've built, you have to burn
it all, slough off the walls like a snake

leaving behind just the bits of life
you dragged all the way

to get here.

# Autumn Madness

Tonight in the dull glow of suburbs
they gather at the edges
of driveways, emerge from shrubs
to scuff their bony hooves
in the windblown leaves
where a streetlamp trickles
its sodium sparks
onto the sidewalk.

One after the other, like teenage boys
testing a new rope swing at a quarry,
they leap into cars' prescient beams
then crumble to the curb.

It's easy to forgive their stupidity.
We've all done foolish things for love,
left something broken on the ground.

The lucky bucks make it across
with just some hair scrapped off
on a fender, driver swerving
and plowing on.

We pass them every day.
Their numbers swelling
like rot gasses
stretching the hairs across
their stomachs.

The survivors gather in dark
backyards and orchards,

crush apples into the grass
and aim their dimpled antlers
at each other's hearts.

# GHOST BARN

She would stand in the corner
of the barn and whisper
love notes to cobwebs,
hoping someone in the fields
heard a vibrato on the wind.

Untouched, the Chevy Loadmaster
with the rotted driver's seat
still smells like an oil can
left in reach to keep the baler
spinning those late August nights.

Once these concrete stalls
held Holsteins' helpless lowing
as barn wasps cleaned
the liquid from their eyes
between shallow diving swallows.

Always work they left undone
as night closed down the household,
a porch still asking for repair,
the south hill field never cleared
of rocks and tree stumps.

There, hidden behind mud daubers' nests,
the note she carved in hayloft rafters
before she left, another unheard
whisper for the fields, seeds planted
that refused to grow.

# Ode to the Half-dead Bear
## on the Way to Defiance

Chained to the axle of a rusted F-150,
bald spots on his sides where he worries
the rind raw, not to escape, just to feel
his tongue roughing blood from his skin.
This road through Ohio's dried swamp
is corn and soy for eyes' miles,
the sun takes hours to set, searching
for the last place it called home.
The hunter who caught him as a cub
in Michigan pumps gas for travelers
who took the wrong road to Toledo,
believing straight lines wouldn't bend,
believing the river was just ahead
where the horizon melts into corn silk's
towhead gaze. This is how he breaks—
the gas jerk tossing scraps of meat
to the Ford's rusted shade, eyes
forever curved toward the dust of cars
pulling out into the road, and one front leg
curled into a crook that never grew
the way it should, the way a dam can turn
the river east, letting water mute
all the land's furrowed voices.
And this is where he'll die, bruised
shadow from Skanee, gumming his paws
until blood is his only memory,
the time he mauled the boy
and watched him crawl away—
the taste that keeps him warm
at night under a moon he doesn't know.

# CATCH AND RELEASE

Wild forsythia lean their yellow tongues
over the cutbank where storms gouged
out the land. Trout that lasted winter
hold below the boughs like wind chimes
singing in the current.

What counts is touch, skin on skin,
not the knife sliding down the white belly,
revealing white meat and blood. I'm happy
enough to know there's fight in life,
gill flaps pumping against strange air.

I pull the barb, bloodless from its speckled jaw.
Fiddleheads unfurl their gestures around me.
Everything that leaves comes back
one way or another. We may touch it all
one finger at a time.

# ODE TO MUTTS

There are no papers to flaunt
a pedigree, no lineage or even
(we must admit) proof
of who the father is—
maybe the neighbor's aging shepherd
who paces the woods between our homes
or that haughty corgi from the dog park.
What matters is the heart
the vet tells us, that faintly murmurs
like a far-off high school marching band
out of sync and stepping on each other's heels,
but proud and red-cheeked with chill
because their families cheer
through each knee lift and turn,
through the tuba's strained honk,
and the kid with the flag
who will go home to his family
of former band members,
the ones who know
that trying hard matters more
than being born into it,
a talent for tail wag and leap,
for being not the end product
of perfection, but the midpoint
in a long line of accidents,
the crack in an ancient vase
that makes it precious.

# To A Friend on the Loss of Her Son

Remember the last time
we drove to Benton?
How the river seemed to pause
as if looking back
at something behind us.
I thought of hunting
by the river bank,
the way wind drives waves
up current and cormorants
disappear into them
then rise, wings open
back to the trees.

You said the boy was dying,
skin thinning like moth wings
under light.
You scanned the tree tops
through the car window
trying to find the eagle
I said had nested here
years before.
Your face flattened against
the glass, like the old
who have lost hope
their memories will last.
It was all I could do
not to stop the car
right then, take you
across the field
to the patch of woods

where I hunted grouse
and show you how wind
lays out a path
through the trees
that all birds recognize.

When we buried him
I thought your face
would crack from the strain
of wanting more, to need,
and needing, understand
what we'd been doing wrong
all our lives to let
them so quickly fall apart.
We watched the light crawl away
beyond the hills
in its daily wish
to put the day behind it,
thinking of grief
as the ritual that comes
with love
or believing too much
that each day should be
a simple repeat of the last.

Now I'm driving again
by the river that fills
up the deep divide
between mountains.
I hear a grouse drumming
its wings, trying
to coax a mate
into forgetting its cover
before rain swallows the season.
If you watch the river pause

again by the dam, remember friend,
memory is the best water
covering every sharp point,
overflowing every empty hole.

# Elegy for a Broken Sump Pump

*for Doctors without Borders*

It's not the low beehive hum
we grew to ignore
especially in spring
when the basement walls
wept with each rising
of the neighbor's creek.
Not the sleep that comes easily
knowing some dumb machinery
is knocking back the weather
to keep our old records
and boxes of children's toys dry.
But I remember the day I cut the pipes
and dug the pit to bury it.
The first deep breath of groundwater
and then my work was done.
After that, ten years of forgetting
it was even there
keeping water from rising
to our chins or at least
the back basement stairs.
We neglect the hands
that hold us up,
the steel rail on a road
left to keep cars
from tumbling down a cliff
until it fails
and how ignorant we seem
in our comfort,
the way doctors

killed today in Yemen
while saving someone else
is the first we had heard
their names
and learned all they'd done.

# Sight Casting

It's not art or science,
more like wind, the way it stirs
the hair on your arm,
the light off silver-white scales
and the angles it takes
to reach the coral sand.

It's not the fish, the semi-
colon of its urges, the sudden
surges like a bird stirred
by movement in the trees,
eyes alert to everything
between it and the sun.

It's not the water, or the way
it sways the reeds and lifts
the boat smoothly like a chest
rising with each breath,
the way you hold it before
the cast, patient, unsure.

It's the search, that heat
you feel in your palm
the moment you see all
angles straight, the line
lengthening over water
and your life paused on it.

# Elegy for a Bounced Check

Money matters.
Let's not pretend otherwise.
Though poets prefer to deal
in things that come for free—
the sound of sparrows in the trees
or horses nuzzling each other
in a friend's pasture
do nothing to pay the bills.
This week the dryer broke again,
the car breaks can be heard
for two blocks and I've run
out of chairs to burn for heat.
Money's meant to do great things—
keep the lights glowing all month,
feed the phone, fill the fridge
with eggs, ham and cheap wine.
Now what's a quickly graying ember
to do when promises made on paper
won't follow through?
Those sparrows I thought
so sweet when they sang,
now lay dead under the window
they mistook for sky.
The horses, sick on jimsonweed
need a shot to keep them upright.
If good things come to those
who wait, what comes to those
who wait online or wade through
endless menus on a toll-free hotline?
What comes to those who need?
Hope? Faith? Just more words

for need.
It's time to trade up for something
solid, cash with less spring
and more weight.
A thing that when you throw it
doesn't bounce, but breaks.

# CAMOUFLAGE

Watching two candidates debate,
I thought, I too have a question
and it keeps me up at night.
Outside, deer pass through the orchard.
They pause long enough to taste
the air, look for dangers they
know are there, but not there now.
I have a question, and I keep it to myself.
We go through this again. Fight
the urge to fight, fight the yard signs,
the radio barkers, the fact checkers,
the friends we stop talking to.
I can't tell the deer to trust me,
though I try to show it, leave
apples on the ground for them.
Tell them everything they fear
about us is true, but not now, or not
today. I do have a question.
I tell it to the deer. Why
do we do this to ourselves? No.
Why do we do it to each other?
In the orchard there's a man
in camouflage sitting in a tree.
He's pretending to be something
he's not. He's been watching
all night, waiting for the deer
to eat the apples like a trick
in a fairy tale, and every
child reading the story
knows what's coming.
And now clowns haunt

the woods, and that's
not funny anymore,
so we keep our children
home, no more stories.
I have a question,
and it keeps me up
at night, keeps rising
like an old injury
every season.
You see, we planted
this orchard.
We let the hunter in.
We know what's coming too
but pretend we don't.

# Mapping Mars

We remember what it was before
all mystery dissolved, before robots
crawled every canyon and scanned
its rocks for sea salt. Now we know

the barren shores, peaks and plains
are barren. The stories barren too,
stripped of life as much as oxygen,
as much as water faded into space.

What replaced the water, filled craters
and the planet's lost canals? Illusion?
Mare, Mare, Auroae—dark places
named for oceans, seas of basalt only.

Last night I watched its distant pinhead
glow still red, still war and dwarfed
by Jupiter and Venus, a carved October
moon dragging smaller lights by chains.

I learn the stars' new names, plans
man makes to make them home.
Mars is more than rock to me, more
than dust to track a trail through,

to plant a flag unmoved by air.
What's lost more than water? Specks
of life and something older? You
show me, and we'll believe it's there.

*Mare Erythraeum, Mare Sirenum and Aurorae Sinus are the names of
features once thought to be dried up oceans.*

# ODE TO HELLGRAMMITES

To river bass, you're Turkish Delight.
To everything else, you're
the river's dank nightmare,
a larval thing that crawls
under bedrocks that have
never seen the light of day.
You're no *Tiger, Tiger*
*burning bright,* but
some fearful hand's
mad lab experiment.
If the hand that *made the lamb*
made you, you thanked it
with a bite that drew blood.
You'd pull teeth
from a gift horse's mouth.
Oh mandible, oh prolegs,
oh stench of undermud and fish guts,
cross between Mothra, Jabba the Hut
and Maine's meanest lobster,
when I twist your fleshy tail
onto fishhook, crack
your exoskeleton armor
with a sharpened barb,
don't get mad, get even.
Light the river bass'
hunger with your sticky gills.
Be the bait that gives 100 percent
by taking the bass
down with you.
But if you survive
and make that change

to heaven's fallen butterfly,
know that every sin
your body's marked with
will shed one night
under a summer's full moon
when you finally spread
your wings
like weeping willows
and hunt instead
from the sky.

# First Steps

Celebrating firsts is what we do.
She took her first steps. We clapped
and made a video. She graduated
kindergarten. We made another video.
A cabinet in the living room overflows
with videos, first bike ride, first dance lesson
and then there's all the firsts we skipped
but remember anyway. First breakup,
first fight with us, her parents. First apology
I made from the doorway of her bedroom,
pink walls and her small body wrapped
around a teddy bear. Enough firsts I can't
even count anymore or know what to do with.
Sometimes I count the phone calls, the things she misses
so far from home. How even a simple text message
in November is like an unexpected visit.
She tells me about school, the new city
bright in its unrest, but lonely, the way a room
with only a television playing can be lonely,
some news anchor's exhausted voice
the only thing she hears.
More firsts coming that won't end
with a video in the cabinet.
She says she's joining the march,
heading to the streets, her first time
shouting herself hoarse before a wall
of police with shields and helmets,
for something so big it overwhelms her,
so strong it takes all her friends, arm in arm,
to sing it into the night.

# TUMBLE BROOK

The brown trout of Tumble Brook
are gone, the stone wall
and the stump we used to meet
to rest our backs against at noon
after following ripples upstream
under sycamores, gone too.

Gone the caddis flies, the filament
of gravel they wove on rock bottoms,
the muskrat holes in the mud bank
and the owl we woke one afternoon
from breaking branches
off a willow struck by storm.

It's not the freeway killed the brook,
the new homes on the east branch
or even the frack mine pump that
lights the neighbor's well on fire.
We took the road to heart, yoked
it always through years of doubt

that this could last, and we were
sure, like friends reliving their
their animal rites, our favorite runs divide.
The heavy fog that hides the ripples
on a fall morning tells it true,
each old step is new. The trail is wide.

# Final Poem  (Trail Head)

It took all day to climb
but when we reached the overlook
at the end of the trail
both of us, without speaking,
turned around to see how far
we'd come, how steep the path
and filled with rocks, then
our eyes moved to the mountains
and the wind gap in the distance,
the river below carrying
the world's sediments out to sea,
and the tree leaves
starting to turn over our heads.

# Acknowledgments

*Apple Valley Review:* Nova

*Burnt District:* Autumn Madness

*The Broadkill Review:* Elegy for the Lehigh Thermometer Works 1945, Fishing with Ghosts, Memorious, The Neighbor Killed Snakes

*Bluestem:* Snakeskin

*The Cape Rock:* Holding onto an Electric Fence, Slant Six

*Cumberland River Review:* Ghost Barn, Things She Couldn't Let Go Of

*Cider Press Review:* Ode to Hellgrammites

*Crab Creek Review:* Confessions of a Snipe Hunter, History Lesson

*Gargoyle:* Coat of Arms, Ode the the Half-dead Bear on the Way to Defiance

*Gravel:* Hexenkopf Hill Road

*Hawaii Pacific Review:* Going Back

*The Journal:* Lucky

*The MacGuffin:* Sight Casting, To Read Dead Poets, With Shelly at the Goodwill

*New Plains Review:* Villanelle for the Allentown Punk Rockers 30 Year Reunion

*Kentucky Review:* Tumble Brook

*Pembroke Magazine:* If This is All We Have

*Philadelphia Stories:* Ode to Scrapple

*Rappahannock Review:* Stealing Clay from the Crayola Factory

*Red River Review:* World's End Revisited

*San Pedro River Review:* Cliff

*Soundings East:* Difference

*Southern Poetry Review:* Bluegill

*Storyscape:* First Steps

*Tar River Poetry Review:* Midnight

*Two Hawks Quarterly:* Catch and Release

*The Fourth River:* After the Tree Fort Fire

*Vine Leaves:* Crossing the Lake with Natalie, Dog's First Spring, Nazareth Road

*West Texas Literary Review:* Burning Down the Carousel